WILD DOG ATTACK

by Lisa Owings

BELLWETHER MEDIA · MINNEAPOLIS, MN

Are you ready to take it to the extreme?
Torque books thrust you into the action-
packed world of sports, vehicles, mystery,
and adventure. These books may include
dirt, smoke, fire, and dangerous stunts.
WARNING: read at your own risk.

Library of Congress Cataloging-in-Publication Data

Owings, Lisa.
 Wild dog attack / by Lisa Owings.
  p. cm. -- (Torque: animal attacks)
 Includes bibliographical references and index.
 Summary: "Engaging images illustrate true wild dog attack stories and accompany survival tips. The
combination of high-interest subject matter and light text is intended for students in grades 3 through 7"
--Provided by publisher.
 ISBN 978-1-60014-793-7 (hardcover : alk. paper)
 1. Dog attacks--Juvenile literature. 2. Wolf attacks--Juvenile literature. 3. Wild dogs--Behavior--Juvenile
literature. I. Title.
 QL737.C22O97 2013
 599.77--dc23
                                    2012013442

TABLE OF CONTENTS

Deadly Dogs 4

Tragedy on Fraser Island 6

Dingoes Strike Again 12

Prevent a Wild Dog Attack 18

Survive a Wild Dog Attack 20

Glossary 22

To Learn More 23

Index 24

Deadly Dogs

They may look like the family pet, but **wild dogs** are far from cuddly. Australian wild dogs, or dingoes, are **fierce** killers. A small dingo pack can take down large **prey**. The dogs sink their teeth into the throats of cows and kangaroos. Some even attack people. Their favorite human victims are small children.

Big and Bad
The dingo is the largest land predator in Australia.

Tragedy on Fraser Island

The Gage family awoke at their campsite on Australia's Fraser Island. Nine-year-old Clinton set off toward the beach with a friend. The boys did not get far before they sensed trouble. Two wild dogs were closing in on them. The frightened boys began to run, but Clinton tripped and fell. The **aggressive** dingoes were on him in an instant.

Dingo Country

Fraser Island lies off the eastern coast of Australia. More than 200 dingoes roam the island.

Clinton's father Ross and younger brother Dylan came looking for him. They found him lying on the ground. He was covered in blood. Then Dylan started screaming. One of the dingoes tore at his arms and legs. Ross delivered a kick that sent the dog flying. Then the dingo launched itself at Ross. After a struggle, the wild dog took off.

Ross picked up his injured sons and ran back to camp. Dylan was rushed to the hospital. He would recover from his wounds. But it was too late for Clinton. The Gage family will never forget that tragic day.

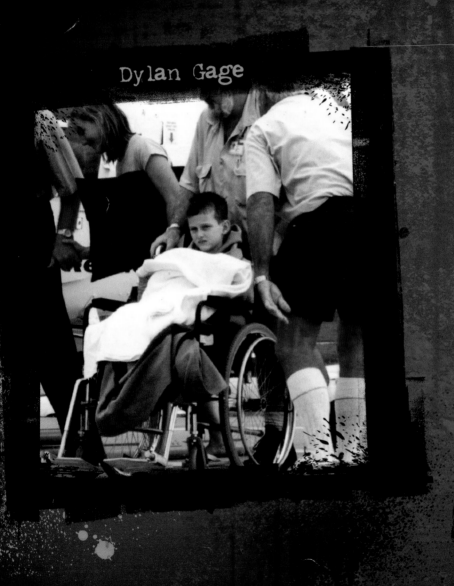

Dylan Gage

Dead Meat

More than 30 dingoes were killed after the attack on Clinton and Dylan. This made some people feel safer. Others felt the killings were wrong.

Dingoes Strike Again

Ten years later, the dingoes of Fraser Island struck again. A 3-year-old girl waited with her family on the sunny shore. Soon a **ferry** would come to take them back to the mainland. The girl went to play among the **dunes**. No one waiting for the ferry noticed the two dingoes crouched nearby.

Within Arm's Reach

Experts warn parents to never let their children out of arm's reach when dingoes are nearby.

A few of those in line saw the girl wander toward the **bush**. Then they gasped in horror as the dingoes **lunged** at her. The rest of the crowd soon realized what was happening. They yelled as the dogs began chewing on the girl's legs. A few brave members of the group raced to scare the dogs away. The dingoes eventually ran off.

"Our experience shows there is only a split second between a playful approach, a bite, and a fatal attack."

—Terry Harper, Queensland Parks and Wildlife Service

15

The girl's legs were bandaged on the ferry. Her bite wounds were treated at a nearby hospital. If the attack had lasted a few seconds longer, she may not have survived. The fierce wild dogs were killed to prevent future attacks. The girl's parents will never again let her out of their sight when visiting Fraser Island.

Prevent a Wild Dog Attack

Most wild dogs have a natural fear of people and try to avoid them. Some will attack young children or people who look small or weak. They may also attack to protect their food or **territory**.

Walk with a group when in dingo territory. Keep food and garbage in sealed containers. Smells can attract curious dingoes. Stay calm and stand tall if one comes close. Keep eye contact. Fold your arms and back away.

No Treats for You, Dingo

Feeding wild dogs can make them lose their fear of humans. This makes them more likely to attack. It is against the law to feed dingoes on Fraser Island.

19

Survive a Wild Dog Attack

Dingo Differences

Many dingoes on Fraser Island have colored tags on their ears. The wild dogs can also be identified by markings on their feet, tails, and backs.

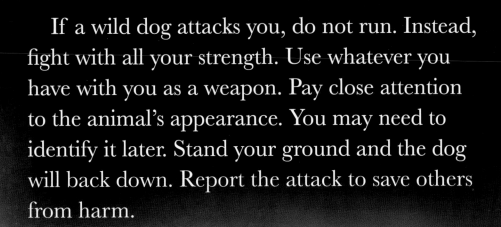

If a wild dog attacks you, do not run. Instead, fight with all your strength. Use whatever you have with you as a weapon. Pay close attention to the animal's appearance. You may need to identify it later. Stand your ground and the dog will back down. Report the attack to save others from harm.

Glossary

aggressive—violent and likely to attack

bush—land covered in bushes or trees; wilderness.

dunes—hills of sand formed by wind or water

ferry—a boat that regularly carries people across a body of water

fierce—violent or dangerous

lunged—rushed forward suddenly

prey—animals that are hunted by other animals for food

territory—the area of land where an animal lives, searches for food, and raises its young

wild dogs—animals that are related to pet dogs but live in the wild

To Learn More

AT THE LIBRARY

Claybourne, Anna. *100 Most Dangerous Things on the Planet.* New York, N.Y.: Scholastic, 2008.

Halls, Kelly Milner. *Wild Dogs: Past & Present.* Plain City, Ohio: Darby Creek Pub., 2005.

Sirota, Lyn A. *Dingoes.* Mankato, Minn.: Capstone Press, 2010.

ON THE WEB

Learning more about dingoes is as easy as 1, 2, 3.

1. Go to www.factsurfer.com.

2. Enter "dingoes" into the search box.

3. Click the "Surf" button and you will see a list of related Web sites.

With factsurfer.com, finding more information is just a click away.

Index

attack prevention, 11, 13, 16,
  18, 19, 21

Australia, 4, 5, 7

children, 4, 13, 18

ferry, 12, 16

Fraser Island, 7, 12, 16, 19, 20

Gage, Clinton, 7, 8, 10, 11

Gage, Dylan, 8, 10, 11

Gage, Ross, 8, 10

identification, 20, 21

pack, 4

prey, 4

survival, 21

teeth, 4

territory, 7, 18